U0609977

中共北京市门头沟区委宣传部编

Ancient Mountain Villages in Western Beijing

散落京西的山地古村落

张书范 丁亥立月

中国和平出版社

散落京西的山地古村落
ANCIENT MOUNTAIN VILLAGES IN WESTWRN BEIJING

目 录 CONTENTS

门头沟区位于北京西部，习称"京西"，山岭绵旦，大河川流，风光秀美，物产丰庶。在史上，这里是向北京输送建材和能源的基地，拱卫京城的西部屏障，连接京城与西北各省重要通道，北京的名胜风景区。考古发现证明，早在十一万年前，这里就有人类繁衍生息，渐成村。种田养树的农户村，烧炭、采石、挖煤的窑户村，守口将士后裔形成的军户村，寺庙服务的庙户村，看坟守墓人繁衍而形成的坟户村。不同成因的古村汇集了不同的文化，这些古村在建筑风格、民间文化、民俗民风上具有不同的特点，构成了京西乡土文化的多性和丰富性。

建筑风格是古村文化的外在表现形式，京西古村的建筑具有典型的山地四合院特点。由地处山区，人们把平地用于耕种，而把房屋建在山坡上，依山就势，开山垫地，在开拓出一块不大的平地上巧妙布局，充分利用有限的土地面积，尽可能地达到最佳的使用效果，而形成了形似古堡的宅院组成的高低错落的村庄外貌。有气派的官宅院、雅致的商宅院、实的农家院，建筑上的精工细巧，装饰上的秀美古雅，突显着山区人民的聪明才智和审美趣。街巷中伟岸的古树、简朴的碾房、神圣的庙宇、汲水的老井、破旧的戏台、闲坐的老，以及宅院内古老的农具、晾晒的杂粮，似斑斓的色彩勾画了农家生活的祥和与恬淡，绘出了世外桃源般的今日景象。

古村宛如一本厚大的百科全书，通过这里的一砖一瓦、一草一木，人们可以探寻到昔日雄关险隘的金戈铁马，古道上的商队驼铃，古庙的晨钟暮鼓，老戏台上的南腔北调，从中取到地理学、历史学、宗教学、建筑学、军事学、交通学、民俗学、社会学的万千知识。

为了把京西古村与自然的和谐之美、深厚的历史文化遗存、与时俱进的风貌展现出来，让人认识京西古村，了解京西古村，关注京西古村，我们编辑出版了这本画册。我们真诚欢迎各界友人、有识之士走进京西，阅览古村，品味风情，享受文化。

Located in the western part of suburban Beijing (or "jingxi," a short term used by local people), the Mentougou District is characterized by undulating mountains, roaring rivers, lush forests and rich produces. In history, this area once served as a key supply base of building materials and energy for the Chinese feudal capital. It functioned as a natural defense in western Beijing, acted as a converging point of the vital routes from provinces in Northwest China, and was one of the top sightseeing areas. According to archaeological findings, human beings inhabited this area at least 110,000 years ago and the earliest mountain villages hence took shape. The villages have shouldered different responsibilities in ancient Chinese historical periods. For example, some villages were specialized in farming, some were specialized in mining, some are home to the descendants of ancient soldiers who stationed here, some were responsible for taking care of the royal temples and temporary royal palaces, and still some were committed to guarding the royal tombs. Different villages in this area have different local cultures, in the fields of architectural styles, folk arts, and folk customs, thus contributing to the diversity and richness of rural and folk cultures in western Beijing.

The architectural styles are external forms of cultures in these ancient mountain villages. The architectures here are typical mountain siheyuan courtyards. The houses are adapted to the uneven geographical features of the mountain as people make best use of the relatively flat lots for farming. Viewed from outside, the houses in these mountain villages look very much like castles dotted on the mountains.

Some are imposing, official residences, some are elegant mansions for business people, and simple houses are for ordinary farmers. The delicate details and beautiful decorations on these mountain buildings bespeak the wisdom of mountain dwellers and their aesthetic tastes. The towering, old trees in the mountain lanes, simply constructed grain mills, solemn temples, old wells, worn-out local opera stages, dozing senior villagers, old-style farm tools, grains on the sunning grounds, all manifest the enchanting tranquility of the remote, unspoiled Xanadu.

Like a thick, encyclopedia, an ancient village offers the visitors a glimpse of its history, the ancient army, the ancient caravans, the old temples, and the time-weathered drama stages. To decipher these remaining traditional cultures, knowledge in a wide scope are needed such as geography, history, religious studies, architecture, military science, traffic science, folklore studies, and social sciences.

To reveal the harmonious beauty between the ancient mountain villages and the natural environment, as well as the unique, multi-layered historical and cultural heritages, and interesting changes in modern times in these villages, we have compiled this photo album in hope of fueling people's interest in these villages. We hope that the readers would some day pay personal visits to these villages and savor the charming cultural heritages and natural beauty of these places and enjoy a memorable stay there.

山地古影

Ancient cultures in
the mountain villages

　　青山掩映，绿水环抱之间，座座古村如同璀璨的明珠散布其中，苍翠的山岗，雄伟的敌楼，碧澈的小溪，蜿蜒的古道，构成了古村与自然界和谐相依的外部环境。

Nestled in the lush forests and high mountains, the ancient villages in western Beijing have maintained a harmonious relationship with the natural environment, from the hills, watchtowers, creeks, to the winding pathways, all being an organic whole.

古村倩影 京西古村多为家族聚落发展而形成，选址建村不但要背风向阳，靠山临水，与自然环境相和谐，还要符合先天八卦的传统理念，以图兴旺发达，惠及子孙。故而一些村庄的整体结构经过先民的巧妙设计，形成了各种象形的吉祥图案，表现出人们对美好生活的企盼和传统文化的寓意，在自然美的基础上增添了人文色彩，形成了古朴的艺术美。如元宝形的爨底下村、龙口宝珠形的黄土台村等。

Mystic ancient villages: The ancient villages in western Beijing came into being with the efforts of different families. The architectures are positioned near a mountain and a river, facing south in line with the Eight Trigrams theory to bring fortune and happiness to the offspring of the family. Some villages have well-designed layout by the ancestors of the villagers today and represent certain auspicious patterns which show local residents' wish for better life and their affinity to traditional cultures handed down for generations. The ancient and simple arts match perfectly the alluring natural environment. The best examples in point are the Cuandixia Village built in the shape of a yuanbao, or shoe-shaped gold ingot and the Huangtutai Village constructed in the shape of a dragon mouth and a round gemstone.

杨家峪村　The Yangjiayu Village

双石头村的石上宅院　A courtyard built on a rock in the Shuangshitou Village

始建于元代的桑峪村天主教堂
A Catholic church in the Sangyu Village which was first built in the Yuan Dynasty

黄岭西村　The Huanglingxi Village

中国历史文化名村—
灵水村（京西举人村）

The Lingshui Village, a
Chinese Village Famous for
its Historical and Cultural
Heritages (also known as
the Jingxi Juren Village;
Juren refers to a candidate
qualified for the top-level
Imperial Examination in
Ming and Qing dynasties)

明代军城——沿河城村
The Yanhecheng Village, virtually a military garrison of the Ming Dynasty

长城敌台 京西古为"神京右臂",从春秋时期的燕国直到现代,历代都视此为军事要地,修建有长城、敌楼、烽火台、关隘以及戍守城池。洪水口、柏峪、沿河城、小龙门、梨园岭等许多村庄都是守口将士后裔聚集发展而成。建村于关隘附近,战时为军,平时农耕。时光流逝,岁月如梭,但雄伟的敌台依然在村边屹立,军城遗迹尚存,成为京西古村一道靓丽的风景线。

Watchtowers of the Great Wall: The Jingxi area has long been regarded a natural defense for Beijing. From the Yan State of the Spring and Autumn Period to modern times, numerous defense works have been built in this area, such as the Great Wall, watch towers, beacon towers, fortresses, and military garrisons. Some villages are home to the offspring of the former warriors once stationed here. Among them are the Hongshuikou, Baiyu, Yanhecheng, Xiaolongmen, and Liyuanling villages. The villagers become soldiers when enemies come and do farming in the time of peace. Time has passed but many of the age-old defense works remain intact, becoming must-see tourist attractions in western Beijing.

位于沿河城的沿字三号长城敌台
A watchtower of the Great Wall near the Yanhecheng Village

敌台内顶藻井
the sunken panel in a watchtower

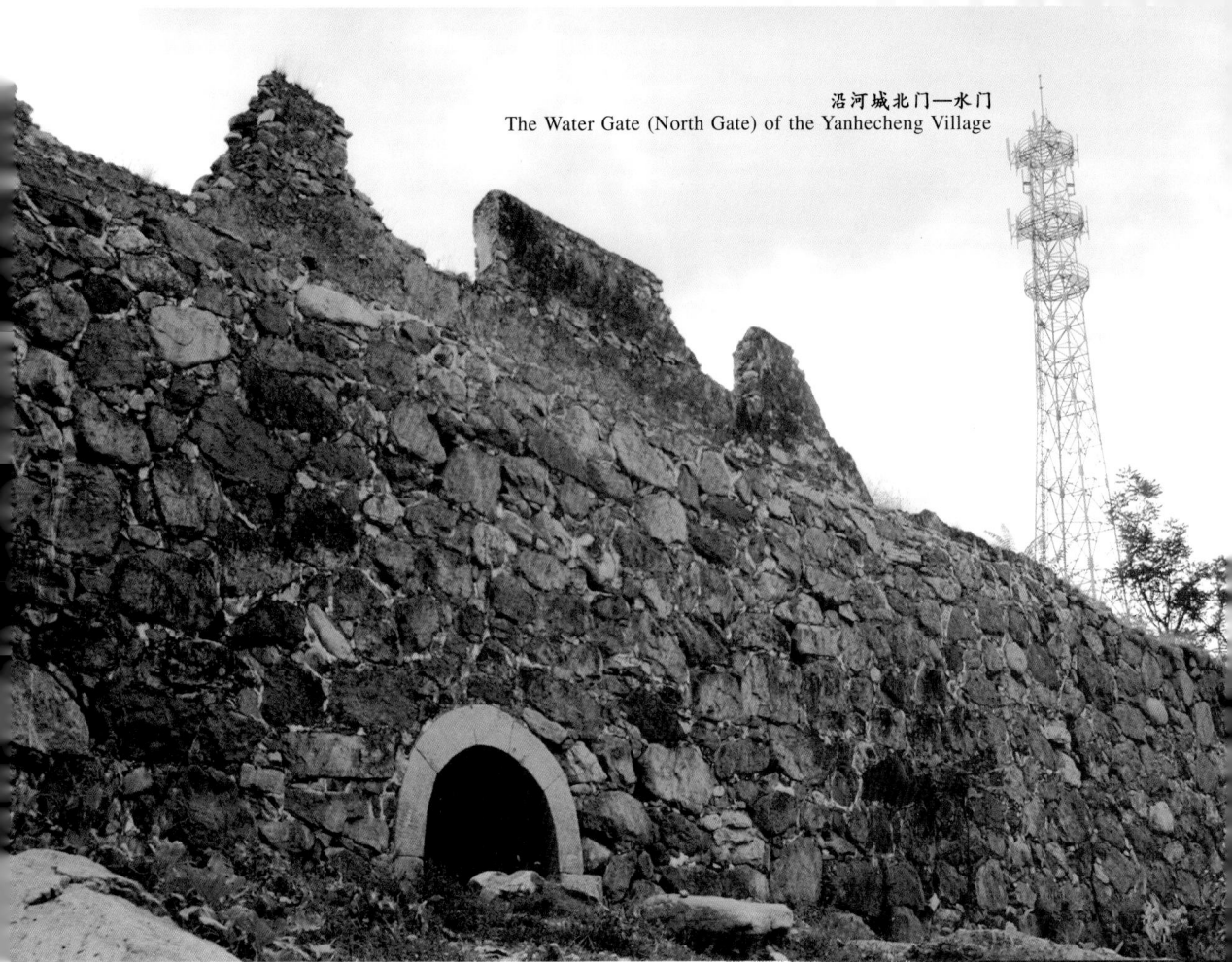

沿河城西门—永胜门
The Gate of Eternal Triumph (West Gate) of the Yanhecheng Village

Temples near the villages:

Most holy shrines and temples are close to the villages such as Pingyuan, Shifo, and Qiupo villages so that these holy places can get adequate supply. Meanwhile, the villagers looking for happiness and fortune can easily get spiritual solace from the holy places. Examples are the Dragon King Temple in Sanjiadian Village, Dragon King Temple in Xiaweidian Village, Lingquan Zen Buddhist Monastery in Lingshui Village, Protector Guan Yu's Temple in Qiaoerjian Village, and Kuixing Pavilion in Longquanwu Village. All these holy places offer local people spiritual support and are an integral part of local culture and rural life. Some have even become symbols of these ancient villages.

村边神庙　京西的寺庙大多位于村边，有的是依庙而成村，如平原村、石佛村、秋坡村等，为寺庙提供粮食、蔬菜及劳务；有的是由村建庙，以满足村民消灾祛难、祈福迎祥的精神需求，如三家店龙王庙、下苇甸龙王庙、灵水村灵泉禅寺、桥耳涧关帝庙等。这些神庙是历史上村民精神生活的寄托，与古村的经济、历史、生活、民俗都有着紧密的联系，同时也是古村的一种标志。

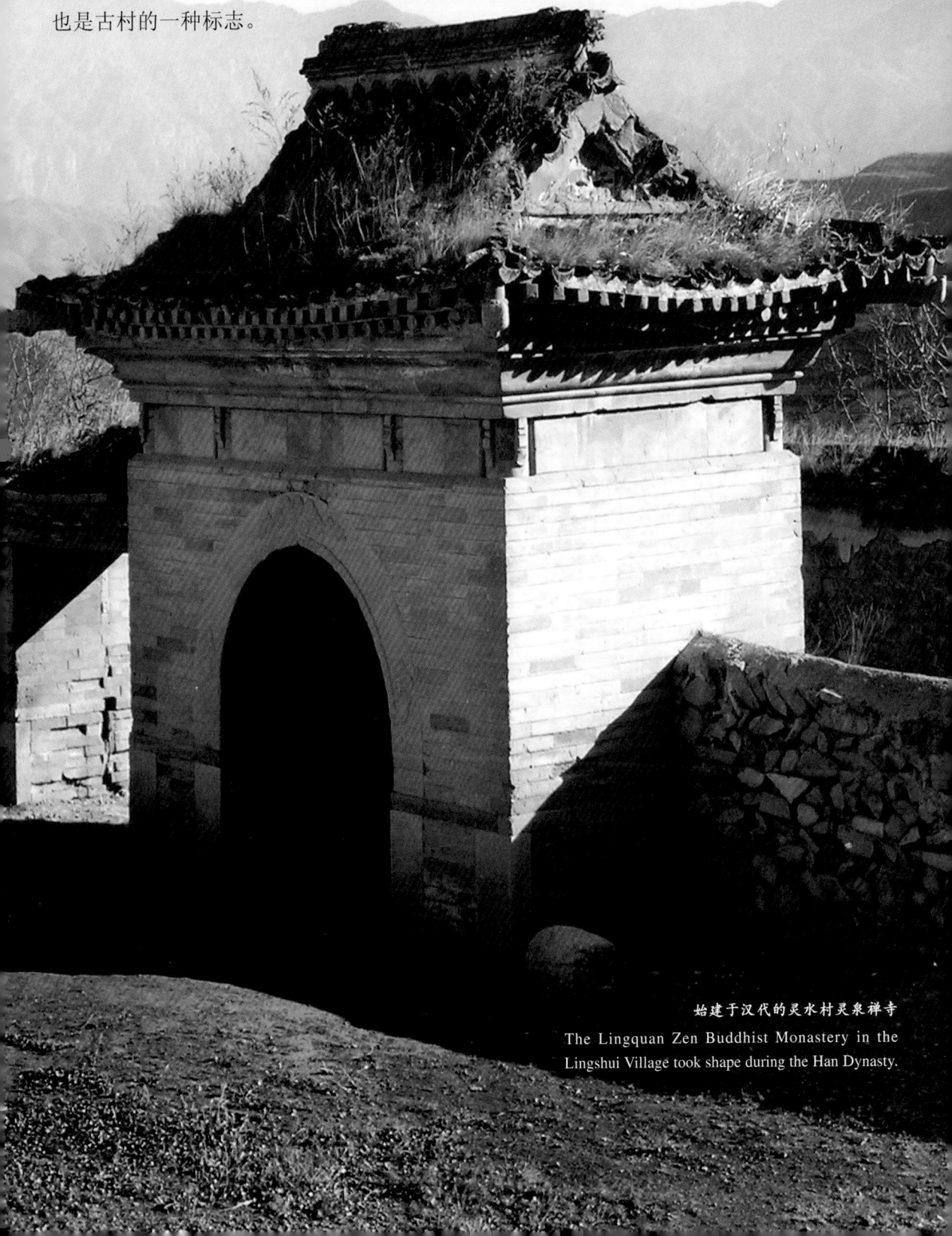

始建于汉代的灵水村灵泉禅寺
The Lingquan Zen Buddhist Monastery in the Lingshui Village took shape during the Han Dynasty.

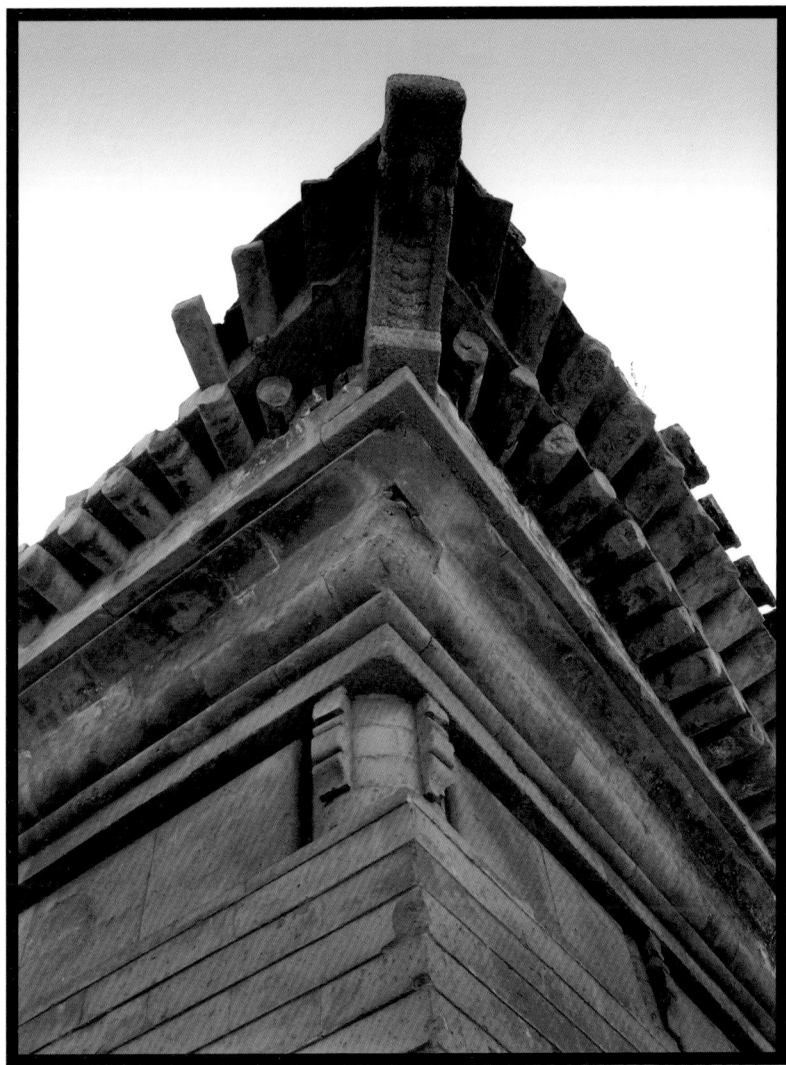

灵泉禅寺山门局部
Gate of the Lingquan Zen Buddhist Monastery (detail)

始建于金代的灵水村南海火龙王庙

The Fire Dragon King of the South Sea in the
Lingshui Village took shape in the Jin Dynasty

建于清代咸丰年间的灵水村天仙圣母庙
The Temple for Celestial Fairies and Holy Goddesses in the Lingshui Village
came into being during the Qing Dynasty in the reign of Emperor Xianfeng.

始建于唐代的斋堂灵岳寺
The dinning hall of the Lingyue Temple took shape in the Tang Dynasty.

殿内壁画
The murals in the halls of the temple

建于清代的下苇甸龙王庙
The Dragon King Temple in
the Xiaweidian Village took
shape in the Qing Dynasty.

46

法輪
常轉

三家店村龙王庙
A Dragon King Temple in the Sanjiadian Village

内殿供奉着永定河神（右一）The inner hall of the temple enshrines the God of the Yongding River (first from right).

保留元代建筑风格的齐家庄灵岩寺
The Lingyan Temple in the Qijiazhuang Village shows an architectural style typical of the Yuan Dynasty.

始建于唐代的三家店村白衣观音庵 The White-robed Guanyin's Temple in the Sanjiadian Village took shape in the Tang Dynasty.

担礼村宝丰寺　The Baofeng Monastery in the Danli Village

阳坡园村娘娘庙　A Temple for the Holy Goddess in the Yangpoyuan Village

蜿蜒古道 京西古道纵横交错，形成了四通八达的古代交通网络，把一座座村庄串联起来。不知是先有的村还是先有的道，许多村庄都以道路命名，例如十字道、官道、三岔涧、四道桥、白道子、道须、岔道等。这里所说的古道是指经过人工修整的官山大道，路面用石块铺砌而成，有用于军事的军道、商旅运输的商道、上庙进香的香道、皇帝巡行的御道等，用途多样。有的沿沟谷而建，有的开凿于山垭，有的凌驾于高山险崖之侧，有的要架桥跨涧。看到古道上那散布的蹄窝，人们耳边似乎又响起了商队的驮铃声，看到山区人民把建材、煤炭、干鲜果品等运往京城。

Winding old pathways: A large number of ancient roads and pathways still exist in western Beijing, linking the scattered mountain villages. Many of the mountain villages have names after the ancient roads and pathways such as Crossroads Village, Official Route Village and Fork Road Village. The ancient roads, built with cobbles and stones, served as major traffic facility for ancient army, merchants, pilgrims and emperors in inspection tour. Construction of these roads took countless labor and resources due to the difficult geographic features of the mountainous area. On these roads, building materials, coal, fruits were transported to the Chinese capital by ancient caravans.

可追溯到唐代的商旅古道（峰口庵段）
A passage of the ancient route for merchants and travelers which took shape in Tang Dynasty (the Fengkouan Section)

西山大道（石佛岭段）
The West Mountain Road (the Shifoling section)

妙峰山进香古道上的万缘同善茶棚
A tea shop catering for Buddhist pilgrims
on a pathway on the Miaofeng Mountain

清代皇帝专用的潭柘寺古御道
A passage of the ancient road exclusively made for the Qing Dynasty Emperors who paid visits to the Tanzhe Buddhist Monastery

古香道边上的摩崖石雕佛像，石佛村因此而得名

The Shifo (literally meaning rock Buddha) Village got its name from the rock carvings featuring images of the Buddhist sutras on the ancient route for pilgrims.

保存完好的圈门明代古桥　A well-preserved Ming Dynasty bridge in the Quanmen Village

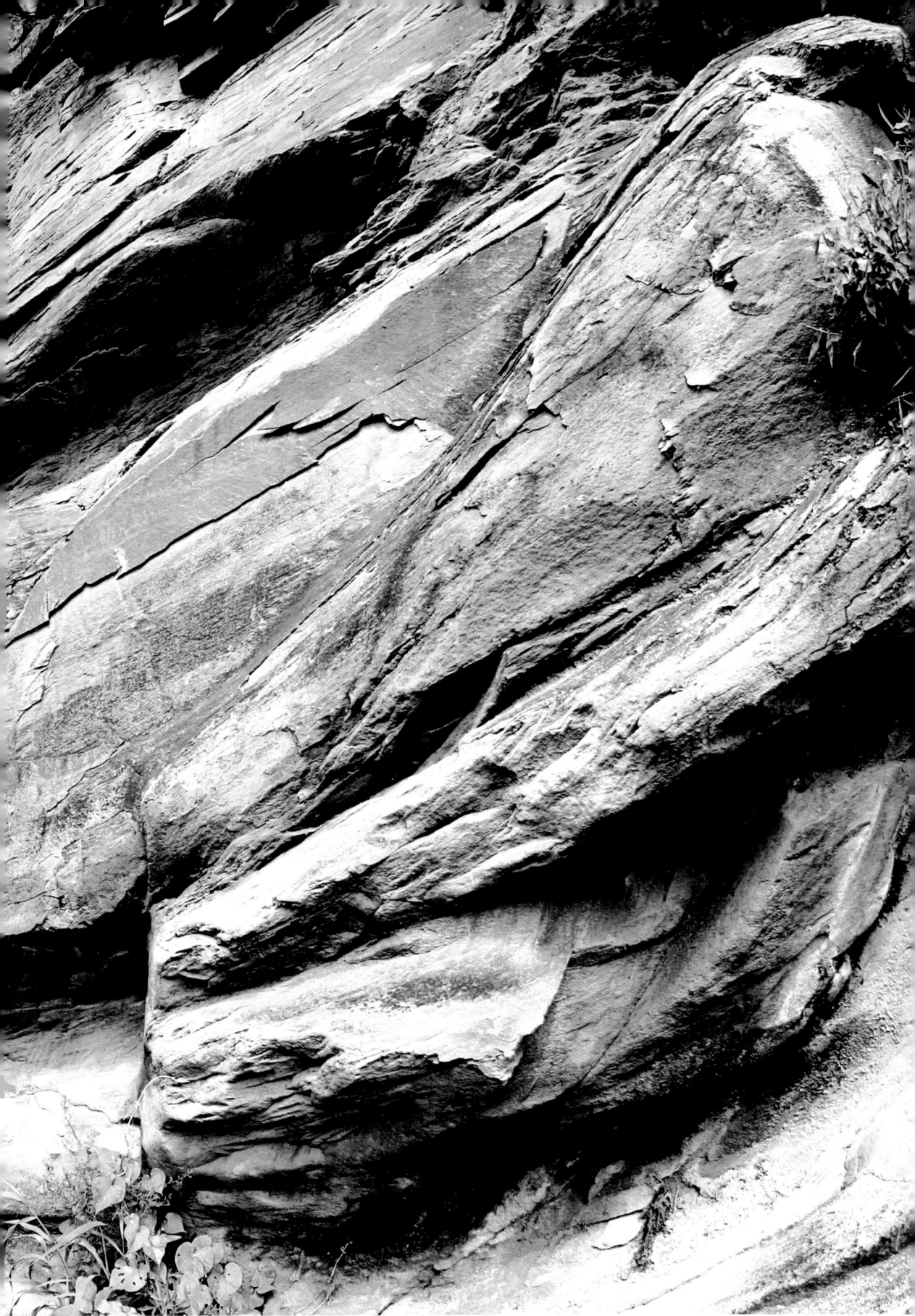

大台古桥 An ancient bridge in the Datai Village

Scenes on the streets and in the lanes

　　街巷是村民日常活动的社会空间，坚固的过街楼、伟岸的古树、质朴的碾坊、临街的店铺、古老的戏台、街上的老井，坐在大树下聊天的老人，追逐嬉戏的儿童，在古村中处处展现出祥和、恬淡的情趣。

The streets and lanes are major public spaces for villagers' community life. The pastoral scenes, from the solid overpass, sturdy ancient trees, simple grain mills, the small shops on the streets, old drama stages, old wells, and chatting senior villagers at the foot of the old trees, to young children chasing and frolicking, all demonstrate the peace and tranquility of the ancient mountain villages.

过街楼 过街楼位于村口，起到防卫和敬神的双重作用，是古村的标志性建筑。有的过街楼上建有供奉神佛的殿堂，人们从下面走过，等于对神佛进行了顶礼膜拜；有的过街楼上面建有值班的更房，下面安装有大门，起到对村庄的保卫作用。虽然现在村庄已经没有了维护，四通八达，但有些村庄的姑娘出嫁，仍要从村口的过街楼走出去，以表示自己堂堂正正地出嫁。京西现存古老的过街楼约有二十余座。

Old-style arcades: The arcades, usually situated at the entrance to a village, serves both defensive and sacrificial purposes. They are landmarks in these ancient villages. Some arcades house holy shrines for passengers going underneath. Some arcades serve as night watchtowers and protect invasion from outside. In some villages, brides will go through the pass during their wedding ceremonies. There are about 20 surviving old-fashioned arcades in western Beijing.

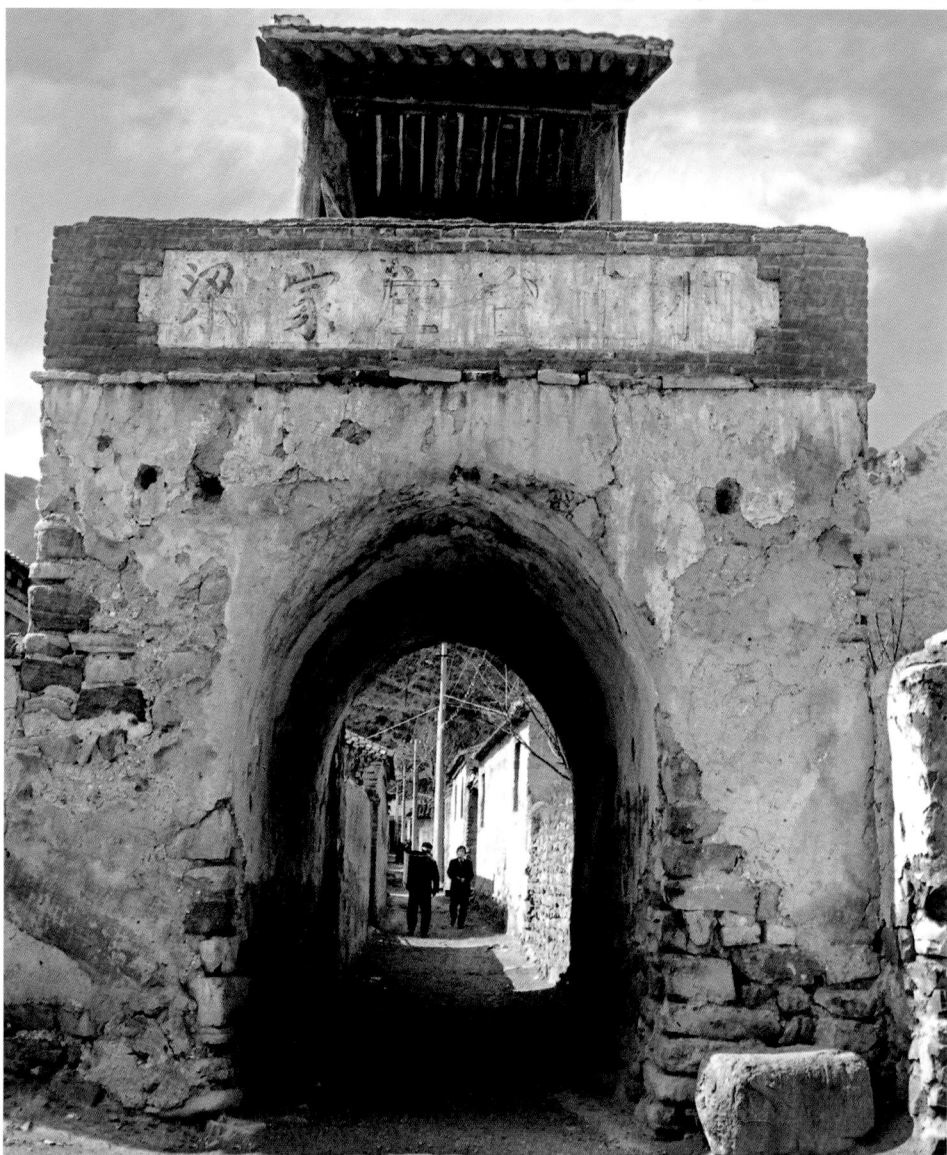

An old-fashioned arcades in the Liangzhuangtaishang Village　梁庄台上过街楼

北涧沟过街楼

An traditional style arcades in
the Beijiangou Village

中国历史文化名村琉璃渠村过街楼
An old-style arcades in the Liuliqu Village, a Chinese Village Famous for its Historical and Cultural Heritages

桑峪村中的街门洞
An archway on a street in the Sangyu Village

圈门过街楼 An arcades in the Quanmen Village

万佛堂村明代过街楼
An arcades built in the Ming Dynasty
in the Wanfotang Village

太平庄（平原村）过街楼，太平庄为康熙皇帝亲赐村名
An arcades in the Taipingzhuang (also known as Pingyuan) Village,
which got its name from Qing Dynasty Emperor Kangxi

被奉为树神的涧沟村千年古松
A centuries-old pine tree, worshipped by local people as a protector, is in the Jiangou Village.

灵水村八景之一 ——柏抱桑榆

One of the eight scenic spots in the Lingshui Village features a cypress twining around a mulberry tree and an elm tree.

古 树 古村的街道上一般都有古树，多为先民所植，记载着古村的历史沧桑。人们喜欢在村中的大树下乘凉、聊天，因而这里是村中的日常活动中心，传播消息的基地，讲故事的场所，俗称"牛皮台儿"。劳累了一天的人们甚至端着饭碗，到这里来边聊天儿，边吃饭。

Anaent: There are always old trees on the streets, eyewitnesses to history in these ancient villages. During the summer, villagers spend a lot of their leisure time besides the trees, chatting. People gather, chat and tell stories. As a result, the cool shade becomes a "Talking Big Stage." Sometimes people gather near the trees, eating their meals.

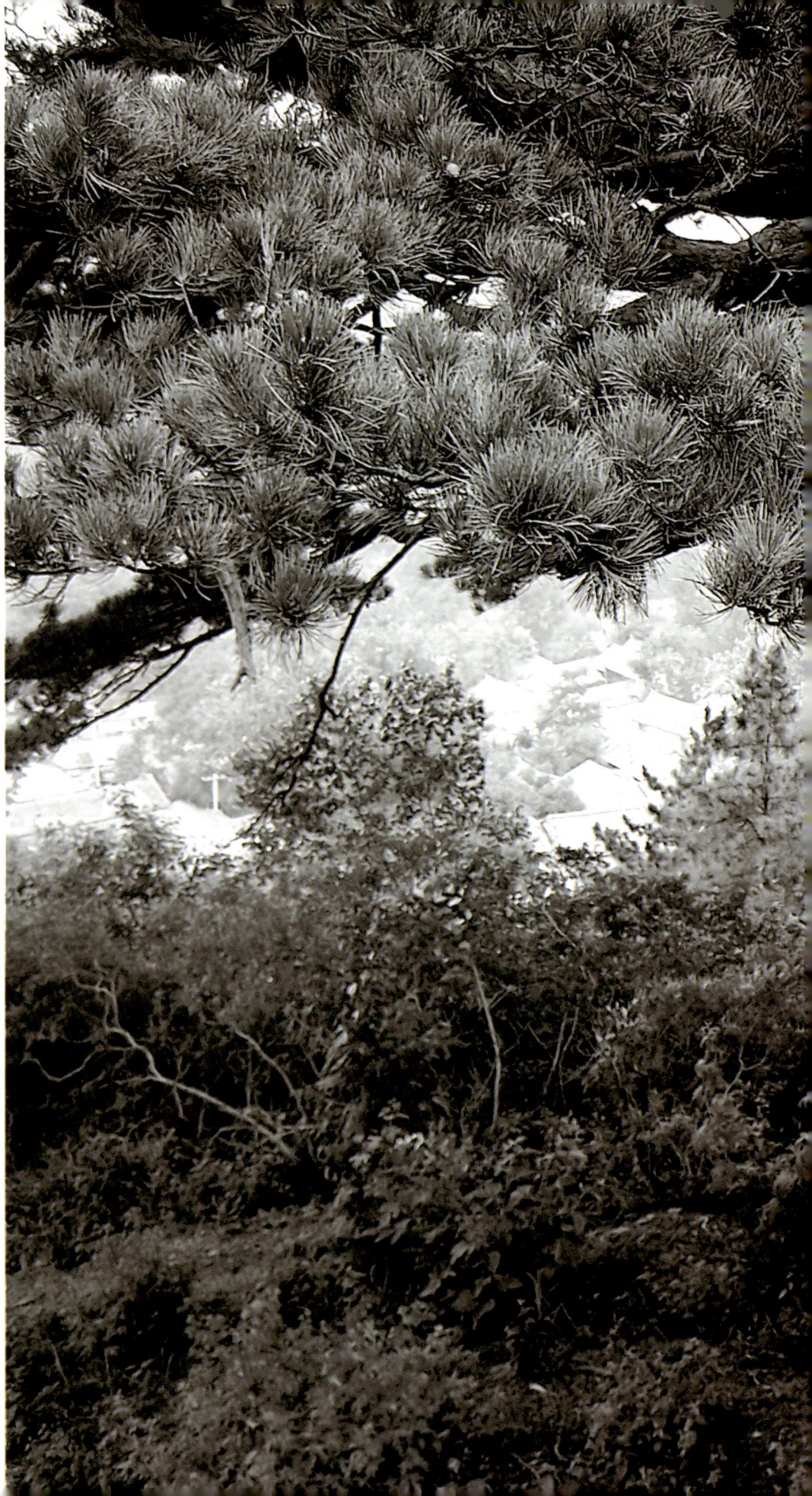

杨家峪村古松
An age-old
pine tree in the
Yangjiayu Vil-
lage

苇子水村古槐 An ancient locust tree in the Weizishui Village

碣石村古槐
An old locust tree in the Jieshi Village

张家庄村古杨树
An old poplar tree in the Zhangjiazhuang Village

石门营村古槐树
An ancient locust tree in the Shimenying Village

大村娘娘庙古松

An ago-old pine tree in the Temple for
the Holy Goddess in the Dacun Village

苛萝坨村银杏树，约有
1800年，学界誉为华北
银杏王

An 1,800 years old ginkgo
tree, rarely seen in North
China, is in the Keluotuo
Village.

黄岭西村木兰芽树

A magnolia tree in the Huanglingxi Village

灵水八景之一——北山灵芝（千年古柏）
One of the eight scenic spots in the Lingshui Village features a thousand-year-old cypress tree.

戏 台 许多古村都有戏台，一般建在神庙的对面，逢年过节、神庙祭祀、喜事庆典，都要在这里唱戏，酬神娱人。村里召开群众大会也在这里。大部分古村都有自己的戏班子，所演的剧种为山梆子、蹦蹦、秧歌等乡土气息浓厚的地方戏，剧目以传统戏为主。尽管设施简陋、行头破旧，但在历史上这是古村最重要的文化活动之一，所以长演不衰。

Drama stages: The drama stages are usually opposite the temples. During the festivals, local operas troupes entertain local villagers while paying homage to gods and deities. Sometimes villagers gather here to discuss public affairs. Most villages have their our opera troupes and the programs, such as Mountain Clapper Opera, Bengbeng Opera, Yangge Opera, have a strong local and historical flavor. Although the facilities are simple, the crops and costumes are old and shabby, the local opera shows have long been an crucial part of rural, cultural life in this area.

张家庄村古戏台 An ancient theatre stage in Zhangjiazhuang Village

圈门戏楼 A theatre stage in the Quanmen Village

碣石村老井
An old well in the Jieshi Village

灵水村老井
An old well in the
Lingshui Village

黄岭西村老井 An old well in the Huanglingxi Village

老 井 水井在历史上是村民们赖以生存的饮用水源，现在大部分已经废弃。井口要高于地面以保证水源清洁，井台用石块砌筑，使其坚固。井口上的轳辘是利用轮轴原理制成的用于汲水的起重机械，井边的石槽用于饮牲口。

Old wells: In the past, villagers relied heavily on the old wells for drinking water. Now, most of the old wells are deserted. The mouth of a well is usually fortified with stones; well pulleys and stone-carved water trough are installed to give live stock drinking water.

爨底下村老井　An old well in the Cuandixia Village

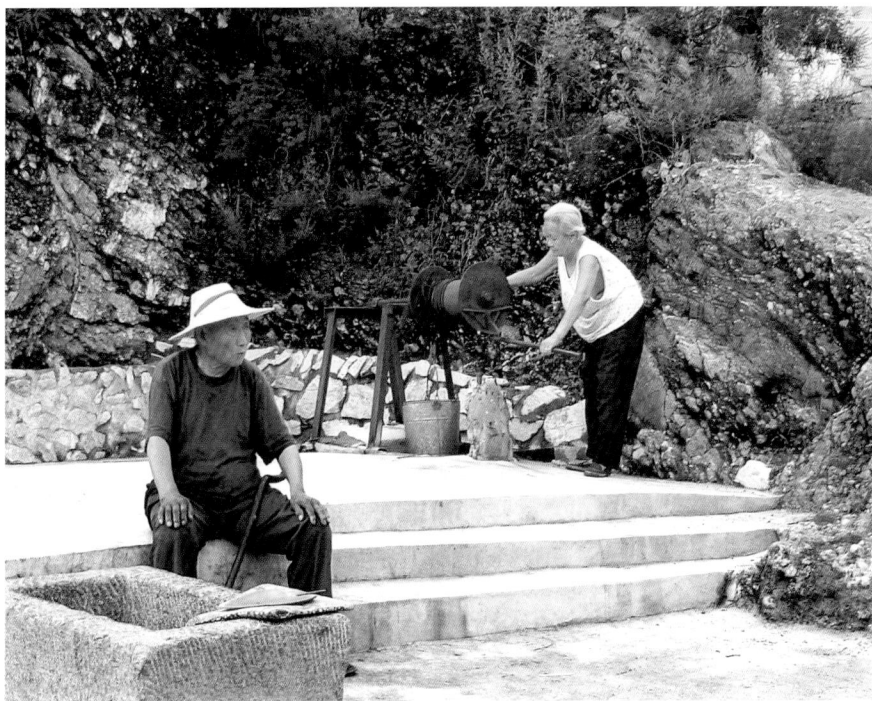

苇子水村老井
An old well in the
Weizishui Village

爨底下村老井　　An old well in the Cuandixia Village

街　巷　宅院之间的通道，宽的称街，窄的称胡同，有的深邃曲折，有的宽敞绵长。大街可行车马，有各种店铺；胡同狭窄，只供人行。从十一万年的人类居住历史来看，京西的街巷可称是北京胡同的雏形，现在是北京胡同在山区的表现形式。

Streets and lanes: The streets and lanes of different sizes and lengths are everywhere in the Western Beijing villages. The old streets and lanes here are the prototypes for the hutongs in urban Beijing, experts say.

杨家峪村 Yangjiayu Village

燕家台村　The Yanjiatai Village

杨家峪村
The Yangjiayu Village

杨家峪村
The Yangjiayu Village

韭园村 The Jiuyuan Village

爨底下村 The Cuandixia Village

李家庄村
The Lijiazhuang Village

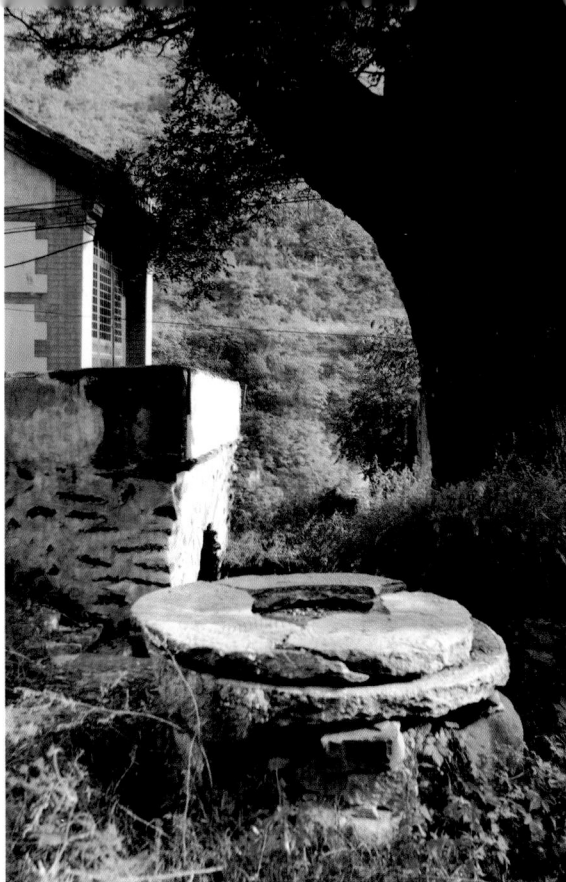

碾 坊 在灵水、爨底下、杨家峪、杜家庄等许多古村还保存着碾坊，石碾、石磨是传统的粮食加工器具，虽然大部分已被新式机器所替代，但部分村庄仍在使用。在灵水、杨家峪的碾坊里还保留着前人提倡相互礼让，遵守先后次序的墨迹题书。

Grain mills: In villages such as Lingshui, Cuandixia, Yangjiayu, and Dujiazhuang, grain mills are still popular. The grain mill, a typical traditional tool, now gives way to electrical equipment.

In some places, villagers still use them. People can still see inscriptions asking people to be patient and wait in order in the old grain mills in the villages of Lingshui and Yangjiayu.

杜家庄村石碾　A stone roller in the Dujiazhuang Village

爨底下村石碾
A stone roller in the Cuandixia Village

碣石村石碾
A stone roller in the Jieshi Village

三家店村殷家大院二进门　The double gate of the Yin Family's Mansion in the Sanjiadian Village

Elegant residential buildings

古建民居是古村传统文化的凝聚点。不同样式的门楼是房主身份和地位的象征，精美的影壁表现出主人的生活情趣和对幸福生活的企盼。四合院的格局表达出主次分明、长幼有序的儒家思想和伦理观念，精美的石雕、木雕、砖雕熔铸着先民的美学思想和高超的建筑艺术，房屋的装饰和室内的陈设表现出房主人家的经济状况和兴趣爱好。

The ancient structure is a focal point of the ancient culture in the old mountain villages. Archways of different styles tell identities and social statuses of the house owners. The delicately made screen walls reveal the house owners' tastes and their wishes for happy life. The siheyuan courtyard layout is an embodiment of the social hierarchy advocated by ancient Confucian scholars and officials. The exquisitely carved stone, wooden and brick components in these ancient buildings reveal ancient Chinese aesthetics and amazing architectural skills and artistry. The decorations and furnishings show, to some extent, the economical status and personal interest of the house owners.

碣石村 The Jieshi Village

三家店村 The Sanjiadian Village

门 楼 京西古民居的门楼形式多样，广亮大门和金柱大门为官宦人家所用，如意门和商宅门为商户所用，蛮子门和随墙门专为普通人家。虽然身份地位不同，但大多都精工细作，门墩和墙腿石的石雕、戗檐上的砖雕、门罩上的木雕，所使用的"鹤鹿同春"、"连年好合"、"福到眼前"、"宝贵多子"等传统图案都有着美好、吉祥的寓意。

西胡林村 The Xihulin Village

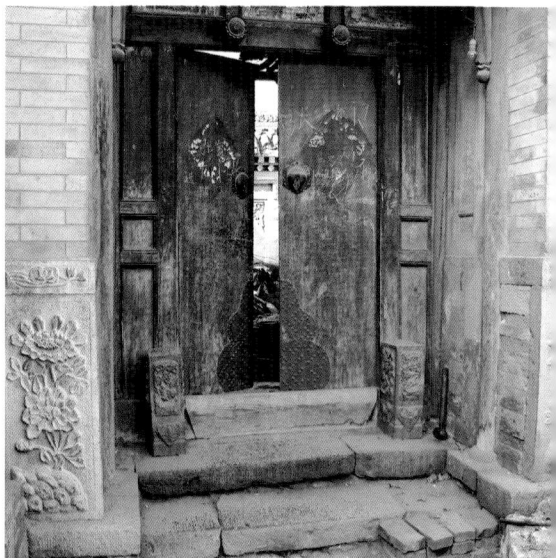

Archways: The archways in western Beijing vary in styles. The bigger, brighter and gilded ones are for officials and rich families, some others are for successful merchants, and still some inferior in shape and quality are for average villagers. But one thing is in common: all the archways have well-crafted carvings such as stone works at the gate pier, the stone carvings at the lower parts of the walls, and brick carvings on the eaves, and wooden carvings on the door shields. The patterns such as "Deer and Crane in the Spring," "Good Luck and Happy Year After Year," "Happiness in Sight," and "Plentiful of Offspring" all bear wishful and auspicious meanings.

石门营村　The Shimenying Village

李家庄村　The Lijiazhuang Village

赵家台村 The Zhaojiatai Village

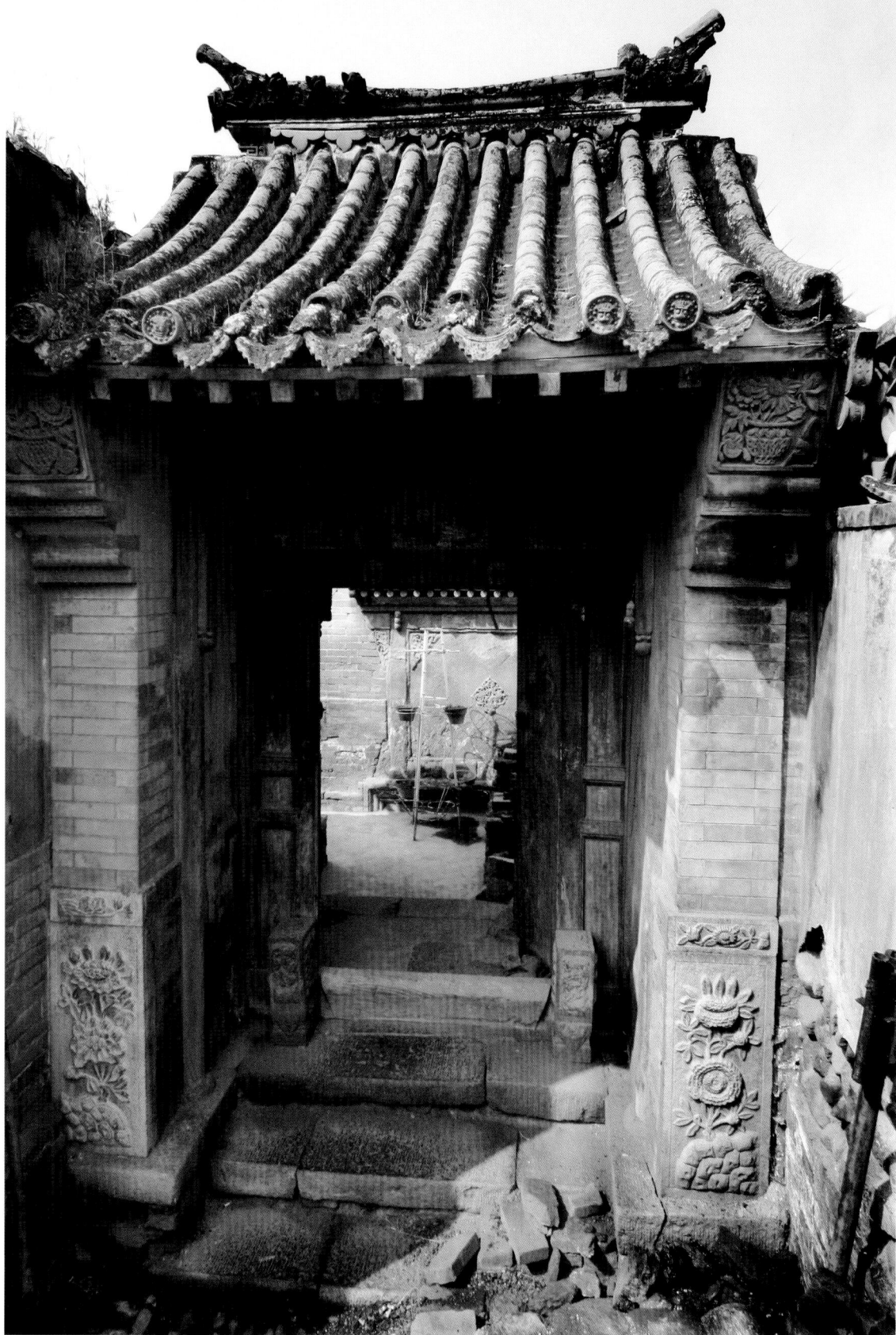

西胡林村
The Xihulin Village

124

石门营村刘鸿瑞宅院雕花如意门楼

The Ruyi-style archway of Liu Hongrui's Mansion features delicately carved floral patterns in the Shimenying Village.

杨家峪村
The
Yangjiayu
Village

126

各式门簪 All kinds of decorative cylinders

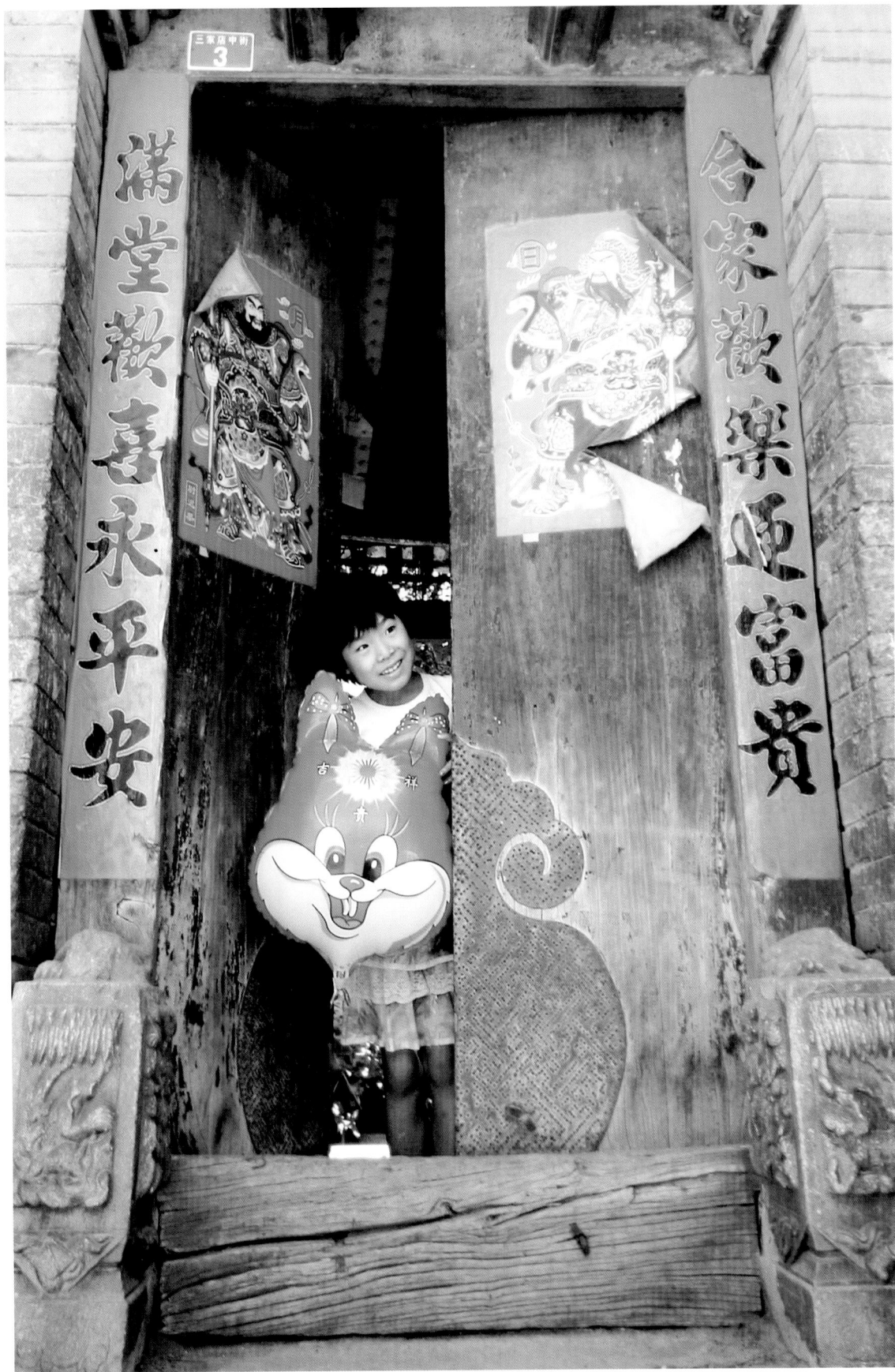

影　壁　京西民宅的影壁分为两种，一种是门前的照壁，一种是门内的座山影壁，以座山影壁最为精美。座山影壁建在厢房的山墙上，正对大门，完全是砖雕作品，正中部分一般为"鸿禧"、"戬谷"等吉祥语，四周和壁顶为精美的砖雕花饰，有"万字不到头"、"福寿连绵"、"暗八仙"等，寓意祥瑞，壁座为须弥座造型。照壁一般比较简单，但上面一个大大的墨写的"福"字，十分具有艺术性，有的用"福"、"禄"、"寿"三个文字或其他代表物体组合而成，或以花朵组成，表现一种美好的寓意，具有浓厚的民间传统文化色彩。

Screen walls: The screen walls in western Beijing have two different types. One faces the main gate and the other is within the house. The latter, with beautiful brick carvings, is more important, bearing auspicious words. The screen wall opposite the main gate is simple. It usually bears one huge character such as "Fu (happiness)," "Lu (fortune)," or "Shou (longevity)," accompanied by floral patterns of a strong folk art flavor.

三家店影壁　Screen walls in the Sanjiadian Village

人寿年丰

靠山影壁
A screen wall inside the courtyard

黄岭西村
The Huanglinxi Village

四合院格局 依照先天八卦，大门一般开在东南角上，路南的宅院大门则位于西北角上。西北是艮卦，艮为山；东南是兑卦，兑为泽，这种设门寓意为"山泽通气"。正房宽敞明亮，厢房低于正房，开间也少于正房，前后院之间以垂花门相连，多进的院子以侧门、角门相连，长幼、男女、上下人等各有所居。

The siheyuan courtyard layout: Constructed in accordance with the traditional Eight Trigrams and Fengshui theories, the main entrance to a rural building in this area usually faces southeast while main gate of a house on the southern side of the road usually points to northwest. The main halls are spacious; the wing-rooms are lower and smaller and linked to the main halls with roofed corridors. Family members of different ages and positions dwell in different kinds of rooms in a courtyard.

灵水村 The Lingshui Village

杨家峪村　The Yangjiayu Village

灵水村　The Lingshui Village

杨家峪村　The Yangjiayu Village

黄岭西村　The Huanglinxi Village

塔河村　The Tahe Village

石板压瓦垫覆顶的山地农家四合院
A typical rural siheyuan courtyard in the Huiyu Village, with tiles pressed by stone slabs overhead

白虎头村 The Baihutou Village

民居装饰 室外装饰主要为影壁上檐、房脊、戗檐上的砖雕，墙腿石上的石雕和门窗上的木雕。砖雕多为"喜鹊登梅"、"鹿鹤同春"；石雕为"琴棋书画"、"富贵牡丹"；木雕的窗棂形式多样，有"步步锦"、"工字锦"、"灯笼锦"、"满天星"等，都有着美好的寓意。室内装饰大多数人家已经现代化，但还可以见到木雕隔扇、条案、八仙桌、连三橱、火炕、地炉子等古老的家具和设施。

Decorations in rural residential buildings: The major external decorations at least include brick carvings on the ridges of the roof, the eaves, and stone carvings on the lower parts of the walls, and wooden carvings on the doors and windows. The brick carvings feature auspicious patterns such as "Magpie on the Plum Tree," "Deer and Crane in the Springtime"; the stone carvings are usually about "Chinese zither, Chinese chess, Chinese calligraphy and Chinese painting"; and the wooden window lattices usually are carved with such auspicious patterns as "Bu Bu Jin," "Gong Zi Jin," "Deng Long Jin," and "Man Tian Xing." The internal decorations today are very modern but traditional furnishings and home equipments such as old-style wood-carved partition boards, tiaoan (Chinese style, wooden, long, narrow table), Eight-Immortal Table (square table for eight people), three-folded cupboard, heated brick beds, and old-fashioned stoves made with stones and bricks are still in wide use.

碣石村
13

供奉门神的神龛
A holy shrine
for the door god

戗檐砖雕
A brick carving on the eaves

抱鼓石
A drum-shaped
Bearing Stone

墙腿石雕——琴棋书画　Stone carvings about Chinese zither, Chinese go, Chinese calligraphy, and Chinese painting

門 墩
A gate pier

精致的木隔扇
A well-crafted wooden
partition board

"紫气东来" "Purple Clouds from the East."

木雕门罩　A Carved wooden door shield

The tranquil, pastoral life

　　恬静的四合院，房檐下挂着金黄的老玉米和鲜红的辣椒，荆笆上晾晒着杂粮、干果，柴房里堆放着老式农具。老人抽着旱烟晒太阳，妇女坐在炕上绣鞋垫，大人们在一起下棋，孩子们在嬉戏，尽显着农家生活的祥和、恬淡。这里远离城市的喧嚣和工业污染，没有商场的竞争和职场的紧张压力，有的是安逸、欢乐、舒适和恬淡，勾画出一幅世外桃源的风情画面。

In the quiet siheyuan courtyards, golden, dried corns and red chilly peppers hang under the eaves, grains and fruits are put above the chaste tree fences to dry, old-style farm tools are piled besides the firewood in the storeroom. Old villagers smoke tobacco in the sun, women do embroidery work on the heated brick beds, farmers play chess, and children frolic, all revealing the tranquility of rural life. Far from the urban centers and industrial hazards, these rural villages have a strong appeal to people who live under great pressure in the cities.

　　Como una herramienta de anotar la historia,la fotografía puede apuntar tanto las novedades como las antigüedades en vía de extinción. BeiJIng es una ciudad antigua de cultura.A lo largo de su histora milenaria,la cultura tradicional venía ejerciendo en los ciudadanos una influencia profunda y extendida,hasta ha llegado a infiltrar en la vida civil. Con el paso progresivo de la historia,la nueva BeiJing se nos estáacercando a zancadas mientras que la clásica va marchándose. Sin embargo,BeiJing ,como capital antigua con historia de más de tre mil años en la de cinco mil años del pueblo chino ,sigue gozando de un alto puesto histórico en la comunidad internacional con su incomparable esplendor.

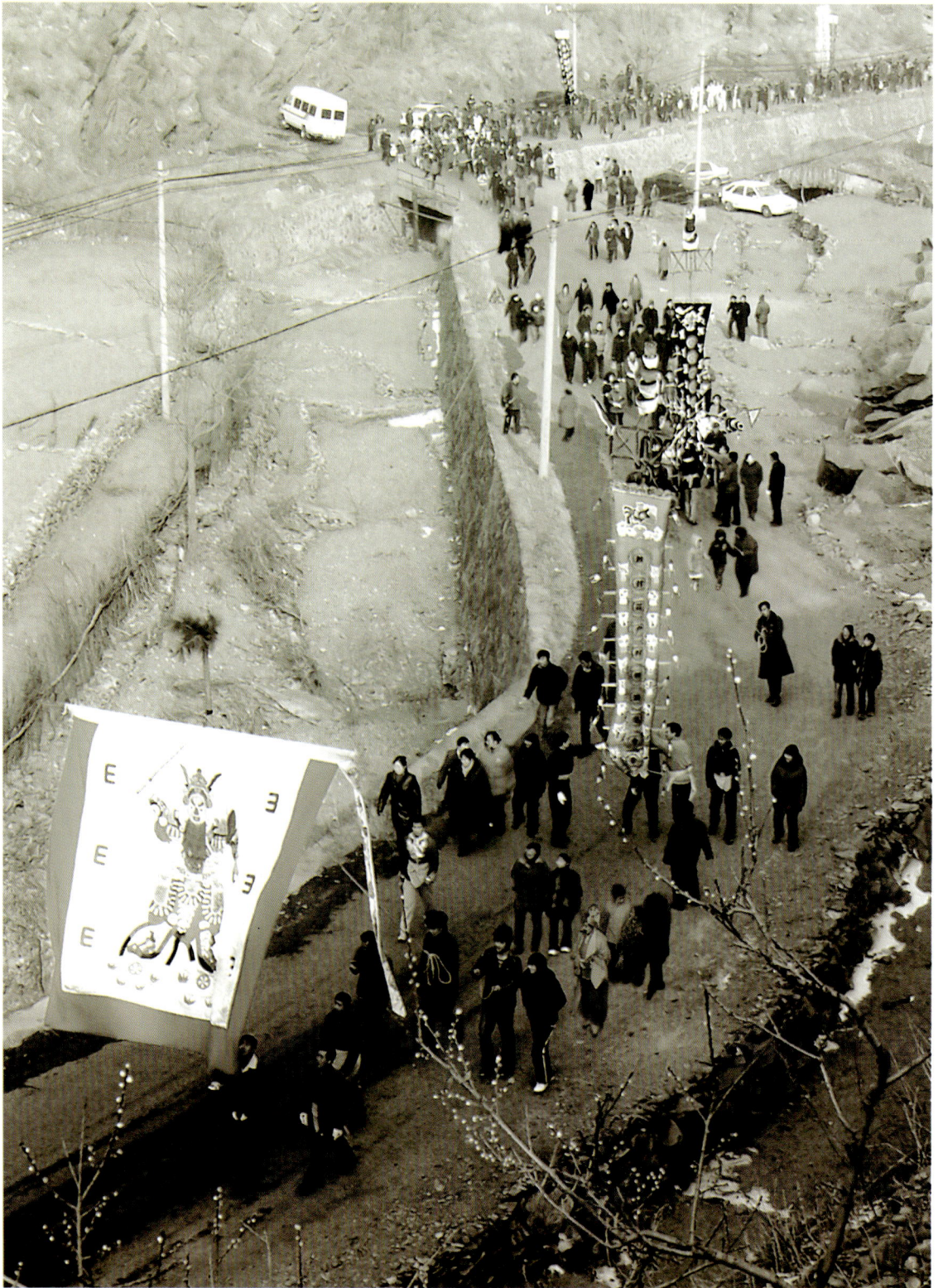

古村
风情

Customs in ancient villages

祈福迎祥的祭祀活动，年节的花会表演，别具风味的山乡戏曲，热闹喜庆的民俗节日，精巧秀雅的编织刺绣，趣味无穷的民间游戏，这是深厚的传统文化、传统的民间艺术、古老的民风民俗所构成鲜活的古村生活画卷。

The time-honored traditional cultures and folk arts, such as the sacrificial ceremonies, variety shows during the flower fairs, unique local operas, joyous and bustling folk festivals, traditional knitting and embroidery, and interesting folk games, in these ancient mountain villages, all together paint a vivid picture of rural life in western Beijing.

龙泉务童子大鼓（入选北京市非物质文化遗产代表作名录）
The Tongzi Big Drum in the Longquanwu Village is among the typical, intangible cultural heritages under the protection of Beijing Municipal government.

双 石　Twin Stone

民间花会　民间花会由古代敬神祭神的香会发展而来，是乡土气息浓厚的艺术表演形式。京西所有的古村都有花会，大的村庄花会有十几档之多，几百年来传承至今，于喜庆节日进行表演。庄户和千军台的幡会、龙泉务村的童子大鼓会已入选北京市非物质文化遗产名录，在京西普遍流行的太平鼓是首批国家级非物质文化遗产保护项目。

Folk flower fairs: The fair, developing from Xianghui, a gathering for ancient pilgrims who pay homage to gods and pray for good luck, features folk art performances with a strong local flavor. All the ancient villages in western Beijing have their own flower fairs. The bigger the village, the more flower fairs it has. For centuries, these flower fairs greet festivals every year. Local arts such as the flagpole-waving shows in the villages of Zhuanghu and Qianjuntai, the Tongzi Big Drum show at the Longquanwu Village, the Five-tiger Shaolin Kungfu show in the Liuliqu Village, and Luozi shows in Xishi and Guyan villages have been listed as Intangible Cultural Heritages under Municipal Protection. The Taiping Drum shows, popular among the ancient villages in western Beijing, is among the first Intangible Cultural Heritages under State Protection.

京西太平鼓（入选首批国家级非物质文化遗产代表作名录）
The Taiping Drum in western Beijing is among the first group of Chinese intangible cultural heritages under State protection.

高跷秧歌
The Yangge dancers
perform on the stilts.

於白村蹦蹦戏演员在化妆
Performers of the local Bengbeng Opera in Yubai Village are putting on makeup.

民间戏曲　京西的民间戏曲剧种多样，主要有皮影、山梆子、秧歌、蹦蹦戏等，柏峪秧歌戏兴起于明初，已传承了六百多年，被誉为戏曲的"活化石"；下苇甸村是北京西路皮影的源始地；山梆子是广泛流行于京西独特的地方剧种；蹦蹦戏是现代评剧的早期形态。京西古村大多都有戏班子，村民自娱自乐，传承至今，久演不衰。柏峪村秧歌戏、西斋堂村山梆子戏、淤白村蹦蹦戏、苇子水村大秧歌戏均已入选北京市非物质文化遗产代表作名录。

Folk operas: The folk operas in western Beijing, such as Shadow Puppet show, Mountain Clapper Opera, Yanghe opera and Bengbeng Opera, have a history spanning hundreds of years. For example, the Yangge Opera in the Baiyu Village originated in the early Ming Dynasty and is over 600 years old, called by experts a living fossil for Chinese operas. The Xiaweidian Village is widely believed to be the birthplace of the Western Route Shadow Puppet show; the Mountain Clapper Opera is a unique local opera commonly seen in villages in western Beijing; the Bengbeng Opera is widely considered to be the early form of modern Pingju Opera in northern China.

Most ancient mountain villages in western Beijing have their own local opera troupes consisted of villagers, and the traditional is alive even today. The Yangge Opera in the Baiyu Village, the Mountain Clapper Opera in the Xizhaitang Village, the Bengbeng Opera in the Yubai Village, and the Grand Yangge Opera in the Weizishui Village have already been listed as typical, Intangible Cultural Heritages under Municipal Protection.

柏峪村秧歌戏 A Yangge Opera program is staged at the Baiyu Village.

苇子水村本调秧歌戏 A Kun-tuned Yangge Opera program is staged at the Weizishui Village.

民俗节日 京西地区民间十分重视民俗节日，除共有节日外，有些村庄还有本村独特的节日，例如灵水村的秋粥节，庄户和千军台村正月十五走会，爨底下村正月十五转灯场，一年一度的妙峰山娘娘庙会，农历四月初八大台地区的福龙山庙会等，都是当地村民最喜庆的节日，是各种民俗活动和民间文化的集中展现之日。

Folk festivals and holidays: The people in villages in western Beijing attach great importance to celebrating their folk holidays and festivals. Apart from public holidays, some villages have their own holidays and festivals. For instance, the Lingshui Village has the so-called Autumn Congee Festival, Zhuanghu and Qianjuntai villages have Zouhui Festival on the 15th day of the first month of the Lunar New Year, Cuandixia Village has its Lantern Walking Festival.

Every year, there will be a temple fair to worship local goddesses and deities at the Miaofeng Mountain, and a temple fair at the Fulong Mountain in the Datai Village. The festivals are considered by locals the most important and auspicious occasions in a year when a great variety of folk culture and arts are presented to the public.

每年立秋日灵水村举办的秋粥节

A Congee Festival is on at the Lingshui Village to celebrate the beginning of the autumn according to Chinese Lunar calendar.

中幡
A flagpole-
waving show

1935年妙峰山庙会

中国民族民间文化保护项目——京西幡乐

The flagpole-waving Music is one of the Chinese cultural heritages under State protection.

每逢正月十五在庄户、千军台举办的大型民间幡会

Grand gatherings for flagpole-waving shows are held in the first month of the Chinese Lunar New Year in the Zhuanghu Village and Qianjuntai Village.

通往门头沟区的主要公交线路
336（阜成门 — 大峪）
370（公主坟 — 门头沟圈门）
645（民族园 — 大峪）
929（苹果园地铁 — 木城涧）
929支（苹果园地铁 — 双塘涧）
931（苹果园地铁 — 潭柘寺）
941（北京西站南广场 — 坝房子）
981临快（莲花池 — 丁家滩）

河

北

省

门

头

房

黄草梁
▲1737

▲东灵山
2303

江水河

向阳口

沿河城

珍珠湖

珠窝湖

碣石

柏峪

燕家台

灵岳寺

灵水

桑峪

军响

洪水口

爨底下

东胡林人遗址
东胡林

小龙门林场
（龙门森林公园）

小龙门

双塘涧

梁庄台上

双石头

西胡林

黄岭西

斋堂镇

杨

齐家庄

清水镇

斋堂水库

杜家庄

张家庄

马栏

田寺

塔河

黄安

百花山林场

白草畔
▲1983

京西门头沟区山地古村落分布图

Map of Ancient Mountain Villages in the Mentougou District, Western Beijing

昌 平 区

海 淀 区

北五环

温泉

建设中的六环路

石 景 山 区

丰 台 区

区

区

沟

区

镇

（台）

太子墓

河南台

大村

淤白

田庄

苇子水

芹峪

妙峰山 1291

洞沟

樱桃沟

上苇甸

安家庄

黄土台

下苇甸

担礼

军庄镇

军庄

东山

香山

妙峰山镇
（陇驾庄）

炭厂

琉璃渠

三家店

五里坨

苹果园地铁

金顶街

阜石路

王平镇

东石古岩

桥耳洞

西落坡

南港

东落坡

九龙山 858

木城洞

大台

庄户

千军台

龙泉镇

大峪

麻峪

模式口

规划中的西长安街延长线

天桥浮

三店

门头口

东辛房

赵家台

潭柘寺

桑峪

平原

万佛堂

冯村

石
路

三

永定镇

卧龙岗

莲石路

南辛房

石厂

苟萝坨

石门营

潭柘寺镇
（鲁家滩）

戒台寺

石佛村

门 头沟区现有1678株市级古树，其中一级古树182株，二级古树1496株，有侧柏、桧柏、油松、白皮松、落叶松、云杉、国槐、银杏、榆树、桑树、核桃树、板栗树、香椿树、栾树、楸树、皂荚树共16个树种。

At least 1,678 age-old Atleast 16 kinds in the Mentougou District have been put under Municipal protection. Among them, 182 trees are First Rank Ancient Trees while 1,496 are Second Rank Ancient Trees. These trees include Oriental Arborvitae, Sabina Chinensis, Chinese White Pine, White Bark Pine, Larch, Spruce, Pagoda tree, Ginkgo, Elm, Mulberry, Walnut Tree, Chestnut Tree, Chinese mahogany, Golden Rain Tree, Chinese Catalpa, and the Chinese Honey Locust Tree.

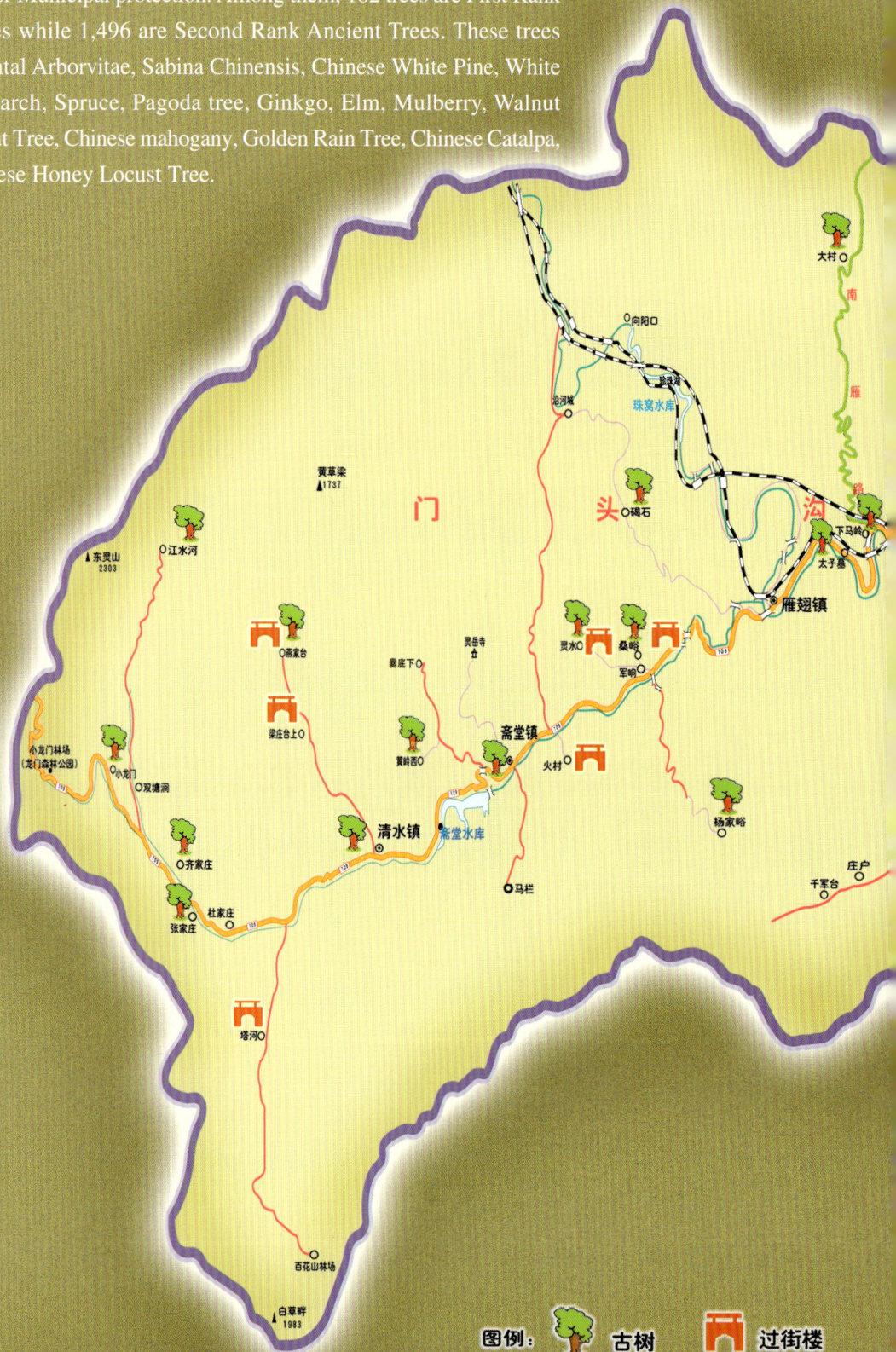

大村

南雁路

向阳口

沧河城

珠窝水库

黄草梁
△1737

门

头

碣石

下马岭

太子墓

东灵山
2303

江水河

雁翅镇

燕家台

灵水

桑峪

军响

梁庄台上

灵岳寺

塞底下

斋堂镇

小龙门林场
（龙门森林公园）

小龙门

双塘涧

黄岭西

火村

杨家峪

齐家庄

清水镇

斋堂水库

马栏

千军台

庄户

杜家庄

张家庄

塔河

百花山林场

白草畔
1983

图例： 古树   过街楼

210

京西门头沟区古树及过街楼分布图

Map of Old Trees and Ancient arcades in the Mentougou District, Western Beijing

▲妙峰山
1291

区

温泉

安家庄

109

109

军庄镇

担礼

军庄

龙泉务

妙峰山镇

王平镇

琉璃渠

斜河涧

香山

大台

九龙山
858

三家店

五里坨

模式口

金顶街

龙泉镇

大峪

麻峪

圈门里

东辛房

建
设
中
的
六
环
路

坝房子

潭柘寺

平原

万佛堂

永定

卧龙岗

南辛房

苛萝坨

右门簧

小园

潭柘寺镇
（鲁家滩）

戒台寺

　　京西地区历史悠久，由于地理条件和历史的原因，保留下了三十多座古老的村庄。古村是京西历史文化的深厚积淀，是民俗风情的秀美画卷。北京市入选"中国历史文化名村"的三个古村爨底下、灵水和琉璃渠都在京

Thanks to their unique geographic locations and certain historical reasons, quite a few ancient villages remain intact in western Beijing. They offer people a glimpse of the age-old local cultures and folk customs in those areas. Of these ancient villages in Western Beijing, the Cuandixia Village, Lingshui Village, and Liuliqu Village, all situated in the Mentougou District, have been designated as "Chinese Villages with Rich Historical and Cultural Heritages."

Unlike the static sculptures, the ancient villages, like flowing streams, are alive and evolving and have witnessed the advent of automobiles, motorcycles, introduction of modern home appliances to local households, and the influx of sightseers from home and abroad.

A roster of institutions, including the Information Office of the Mentougou District Government, Beijing Photographers Association, the Tourism Board of the Mentougou District, and the Beijing Research Society of the Yongding River Culture Cultures, have worked together to present a better picture of the culturally unique ancient villages in western Beijing.

From different perspectives, the veteran photographers have captured the best of the ancient mountain villages in western Beijing for this photo album. With hundreds of photos, the album provides with the readers a glimpse of the charm of these tucked-away villages. We hope that the album can fuel the readers' enthusiasm to explore these villages in person and to find inner joy and tranquility there, staying away for a while from the hustle-bustle of urban life.

We would like to take this opportunity to extend our sincere thanks to the photographers who have invested their time and energy to take the quality photos for this album about ancient mountain villages in western Beijing. Our thanks also go to all other friends who have contributed one way or another to the successfully editing and publication of this wonderful photo album.

The Editorial Board

编　委　会
The Editorial Board

顾　　问 (Advisors)：

　　伊欣欣 Yi Xinxin　刘云广 Liu Yunguang

主　　编 (Editor-in-Chief)：

　　陈志强 Chen Zhiqiang

副 主 编 (Deputy Editior-in-Chief)：

　　衣丰飞 Yi Fengfei

编　　委 (Editors)：

(以姓氏笔画为序 in order of the strokes in Chinese characters)

王　越 Wang Yue	王　媛 Wang Yuan	石　军 Shi Jun
刘德泉 Liu Dequan	衣丰飞 Yi Fengfei	吕小中 Lu Xiaozhong
任全礼 Ren Quanli	李英杰 Li Yingjie	李争三 Li Zhengsan
李雪莲 Li Xuelian	陈志强 Chen Zhiqiang	陈世杰 Chen Shijie
张广林 Zhang Guanglin	张守玉 Zhang Shouyu	张慧军 Zhang Huijun
袁树森 Yuan Shusen	崔兴珠 Cui Xingzhu	琚小红 Ju Xiaohong

撰　　稿 (Language supervisor)：

　　袁树森 Yuan Shusen

装帧设计 (Designer)：

　　吕小中 Lu Xiaozhong

责任编辑 (Executive editor)：

　　杨　都 Yang Du　李路 Li Lu

英文翻译 (English translator)：

　　朱林勇 Zhu Linyong

图片作者（以姓氏笔画为序）：
Photographers(in order of the strokes in Chinese characters):

刁立声 Diao Lisheng	于晓文 Yu Xiaowen	马天杰 Ma Tianjie	马大猷 Ma Dayou
王 丽 Wang Li	王书慧 Wang Shuhui	王金贤 Wang Jinxian	王希宝 Wang Xibao
王秀敏 Wang Xiumin	王燕芬 Wang Yanfen	韦有元 Wei Youyuan	申晓辉 Shen Xiaohui
艾天庆 Ai Tianqing	兰先策 Lan Xiance	许 评 Xu Ping	吕小中 Lu Xiaozhong
曲 扬 Qu Yang	刘泉库 Liu Quanku	刘立军 Liu Lijun	刘德泉 Liu Dequan
刘敏秀 Liu Minxiu	孙惠泉 Sun Huiquan	朱士安 Zhu Shian	朱天纯 Zhu Tianchun
朱京秋 Zhu Jingqiu	李长山 Li Changshan	李英杰 Li Yingjie	李英凯 Li Yingkai
李增启 Li Zengqi Li	苏林重 Su Linzhong	李 涛 Li Tao	李玉峰 Li Yufeng
李争三 Li Zhengsan	李志昌 Li Zhichang	李艳苹 Li Yanping	李 慧 Li Hui
佟西正 Tong Xizheng	吴国才 Wu Guocai	吴建国 Wu Jianguo	吴建骅 Wu Jianhua
陈玉昌 Chen Yuchang	陈仲德 Chen Zhongde	陈梅芳 Chen Meifang	金 华 Jin Hua
杨少军 Yang Shaojun	杨荣兴 Yang Rongxing	杨振武 Yang Zhenwu	易国跃 Yi Guoyue
张小义 Zhang Xiaoyi	张德文 Zhang Dewen	张殿英 Zhang Dianying	张锁安 Zhang Suoan
周瑞增 Zhou Ruizeng	周明星 Zhou Mingxing	赵 辉 Zhao Hui	赵 莉 Zhao Li
赵伯阳 Zhao Boyang	庞铮铮 Pang Zhengzheng	姚宝良 Yao Baoliang	姚金才 Yao Jincai
胖美云 Pang Meiyun	荆惠芝 Xing Huizhi	徐正荣 Xu Zhengrong	高国樑 Gao Guoliang
高俊英 Gao Junying	梁国喜 Liang Guoxi	梁春生 Liang Chunsheng	詹京建 Zhan Jingjian
魏 刚 Wei Gang			

支持单位（Supporting organizations）：

中国新闻摄影协会 Chinese Photojournalists Association
北京摄影家协会 Beijing Photographers Association
北京青年报 Beijing Youth Daily
北京卷烟厂 Beijing Cigarette Factory
北京交通台 Beijing Traffic Radio
北京永定河文化研究会 Beijing Yongding River Culture Research Society

图书在版编目（CIP）数据

散落京西的山地古村落 / 陈志强主编. —北京：中国
和平出版社，2008.1
ISBN 978-7-80201-695-8

Ⅰ.散··· Ⅱ.陈··· Ⅲ.村落－概况－门头沟区－摄影集
Ⅳ.K921.3-64

中国版本图书馆CIP数据核字（2008）第008727号

散 落 京 西 的 山 地 古 村 落
中共北京市门头沟区委宣传部 编

责任编辑：杨都　李路
装帧设计：吕小中
监　　印：王红　宋小仓

出版发行　**中国和平出版社**
社　　址：北京市西城区鼓楼西大街154号　（100009）
发 行 部：(010) 84026161
网　　址：www.hpbook.com
E－mail：hpbook@hpbook.com
经　　销：新华书店
印　　刷：北京盛兴文豪彩色印刷有限公司

开　　本：180毫米×260毫米　　1/16
印　　张：14
版　　次：2008年1月第1版　　2008年1月第1次印刷
印　　数：1—10,000 册

（版权所有　侵犯必究）

ISBN 978-7-80201-695-8/G·552　　　定价：160.00元

（本书如有印装质量问题，请与我社发行部联系退换）